Cover illustration: US paratroopers of the 82nd Airborne Division prepare to jump on Salerno in September 1943. The distinctive colour of the parachutist's utilities and the brown jump boots are clearly seen. (US Army)

1. In April 1941, members of the 501st Parachute Battalion, which was the first regular airborne infantry unit in the US Army, complete a practice jump at Fort Benning, Georgia. (US Army)

US SPECIAL FORCES
of World War Two
LEROY THOMPSON

ARMS AND ARMOUR PRESS
London – Melbourne – Harrisburg, Pa. – Cape Town

Introduction

Uniforms Illustrated 1: US Special Forces of World War Two
Published in 1984 by
Arms and Armour Press, Lionel Leventhal Limited,
2–6 Hampstead High Street, London NW3 1QQ;
4–12 Tattersalls Lane, Melbourne, Victoria 3000,
Australia; Sanso Centre, 8 Adderley Street,
PO Box 94, Cape Town 8000, South Africa;
Cameron and Kelker Streets, PO Box 1831,
Harrisburg, Pennsylvania 17105, USA.

British Library Cataloguing in Publication Data:
Thompson, Leroy
U.S. Special Forces of World War Two.—(Uniforms
illustrated; 1)
1. United States. *Army. Special Forces*
2. World War, 1939–1945—Campaigns
I. Title   II. Series
940.54′12′73   D769.31
ISBN 0-85368-624-6

Edited by Michael Boxall.
Layout by Roger Chesneau.
Typeset by CCC, printed and bound in Great Britain
by William Clowes Limited, Beccles and London.

Elite forces, in the sense the term is now used, really came into existence during the Second World War. In the United States, the Parachute Test Platoon formed in 1940 would evolve into five airborne divisions by the end of the war five years later. These paratroopers would spearhead virtually every major landing during the reconquest of Europe and would play an important part in recapturing the Philippines. Not all US airborne troops floated into battle suspended beneath a parachute, however. Gliderborne troops, especially artillerymen, were an important part of US airborne striking power as well.

The successes of the British Commandos convinced US military planners of the need for another élite unit which could carry out amphibious raids. As a result the US Army Rangers and US Marine Raiders were formed and trained to raid enemy coasts. The Marines also formed their own parachute and glider troops.

Foreseeing the need for élite troops capable of fighting in mountains or in the Arctic regions of Norway, two US units were formed and trained for mountain or ski operations. The 1st Special Service Force was a very tough unit of Americans and Canadians, trained as commandos, ski troops, mountain troops, and paratroopers. The 10th Mountain Division, on the other hand, was trained along the lines of European Alpine units and saw action in the mountains of Italy.

Two other US élite units which should be mentioned are the OSS, which carried out missions behind enemy lines, organizing and training the Resistance, and Merrill's Marauders who carried out deep penetration missions behind Japanese lines.

All of these units had a valid claim to the title of 'Elite Unit' and in many cases their distinctive paratrooper boots, insignia, or special daggers set them apart from their more conventional comrades.

Leroy Thompson, 1984

2. Soldiers of the 1st SSF practising belaying techniques in the Rockies; the parkas are reversible, the other side being white for camouflage in snow. (US Army)

▲3

3. Men of the 501st Parachute Battalion leaving the drop zone after a practice jump in April 1941, offer a good view of how light US paratroopers jumped in the early days. Note the baggy jump coverall (originally aircraft mechanic's coveralls) and the A-2 cloth flying helmet. (US Army)
4. Troops of the 501st Parachute Battalion prepare for a jump in April 1941. This photograph offers a good view of the cloth flying helmet worn by early US paratroopers and of the special leather boots issued to the Parachute Test Platoon and the members of the 501st Parachute Battalion. Parachutes are the T-4. The man passing in the foreground is Lieutenant William Ryder who commanded the Parachute Test Platoon which was the basis for the 501st Parachute Battalion. The aircraft appears to be a C-33. (US Army)

▼4

5. Troops of the 501st Parachute Battalion retrieve their M1 Garand rifles from the equipment roll which was dropped separately. Later US paratroopers would jump with their weapons, but in the early days the German practice of jumping with only a pistol was followed. (Note the 1911 .45 automatic worn on the hip of the man at the left.) M36 belts are worn to carry clips for the M1s. (US Army)

6. A paratroop captain inspects chutes, April 1941. Note his paratrooper's cap insignia. This photograph affords a good view of the A-2 helmet and coverall. (US Army)

6▼

7. Pilot's goggles worn with the flying helmet by aircrew were also sometimes used by the early paratroopers, as can be seen here. Large cargo pockets in the jump coverall were also quite useful. (US Army)

8. Jumpmaster checking the deployment bag on a member of the 501st Parachute Battalion's reserve chute prior to a jump in April 1941. (US Army)

9. A trooper of the 105th Parachute Battalion, undergoing training at Fort Benning, jumps from the 250ft tower. Until the towers were built at Fort Benning, early trainees were flown to Hightstown, New Jersey to jump from the towers there. (US Army)

9▶

10. A trainee paratrooper being strapped into the harness before a tower jump in October 1942. (US Army)

▲11

11. US Rangers undergoing training with British Commandos in Scotland during the summer of 1942. Helmets appear to be US ME1 or British Mk 1. The soldier in the right foreground is armed with a Browning Automatic Rifle, the man behind him has an M1 Garand. (US Army)

12. A US Ranger covered with mud after completing the obstacle course at the British Commando Depot at Achnacarry. (US Army)

13. US Rangers on a speed march in North Africa late in 1942. The central figure is LTC William Darby. The US Mk 1 helmet is now worn by the Rangers, the British-style helmet apparently having been used only while training with the Commandos. (US Army)

◀12　　　　13▶

15▲

14. Colonel William Darby, who commanded the US Rangers, often used the motorcycle seen here in North Africa. Like many Rangers, Darby favoured the O3A3 Springfield rifle for its long-range accuracy and carried one in the scabbard mounted on his cycle. Seemingly a remnant of Commando training, the Ranger in the foreground wears an F-S Commando dagger between his first aid kit and pistol. (US Army)

15. US Rangers training on the obstacle course late in 1942. (US Army)

16. As with the Commandos, the Rangers specialized in unarmed combat training. Note the gaiters and side caps. (US Army)

◀16

17. Rangers on a forced march in Algeria move over an embankment. Note that only the light haversack is worn and that the Ranger in the right foreground carries a climbing rope. Once again like the Commandos, the Rangers emphasised scaling techniques in their training. (US Army)

18. US Rangers moving through a village in Algeria in 1943. (US Army)

19. A. Cap insignia for glider/paratroops: red border indicates artillery; blue border, infantry. The direction the glider is pointing in indicates that both of these are enlisted insignia.

B. Paratroop cap insignia: red for artillery; blue, infantry.
C. Glider troops cap badges: light blue background indicates infantry; both red background and red border are for artillery. Light blue badge on the left is for officers, the other two are for enlisted personnel. **D.** SSI of Airborne Command. **E.** Pocket insignia of the 506th PIR. **F.** Pocket insignia of the 511th PIR. **G.** Pocket insignia of the 508th PIR. **H.** Pocket insignia of the 511th PIR. **I.** Pocket insignia of the 501st PIR. **J.** Pocket insignia of the 127th Airborne Engineers. **K.** Post-Corregidor pocket insignia of the 503rd PIR. **L.** Pocket insignia of the 505th PIR.

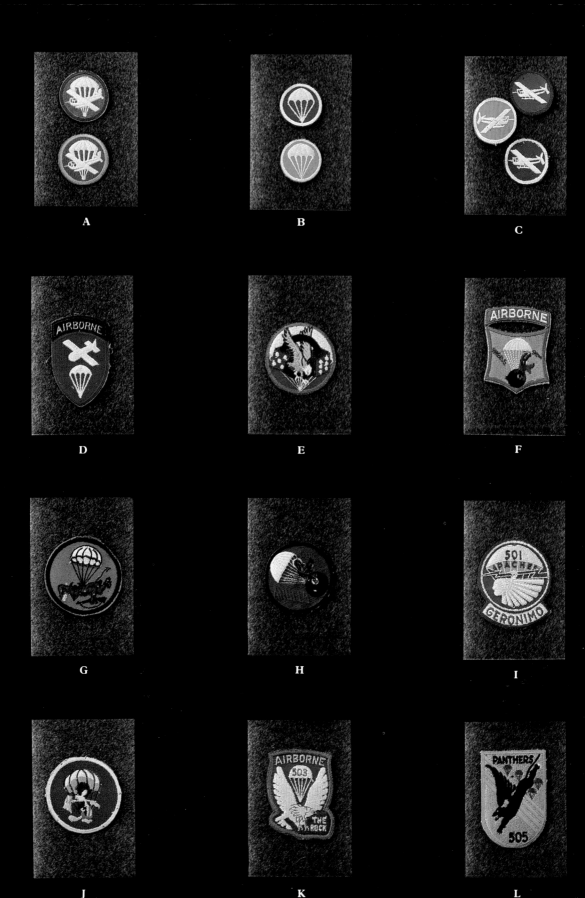

A

B

C

D

E

F

G

H

I

J

K

L

A

B

C

D

E

F

G

H

I

J

K

L

20. A. First Special Service Force SSI. **B.** US Marine Raider SSI. **C.** US Marine Parachute Troops SSI. **D.** 5307th Composite Unit (Merrill's Marauders) insignia adopted after the operation behind Japanese lines. **E.** Insignia of the OSS-trained Jingpaw Rangers. **F.** 10th Mountain Division SSI. **G.** 11th Airborne Division SSI. **H.** 13th Airborne Division SSI. **I.** 17th Airborne Division SSI. **J.** 82nd Airborne Division SSI. **K.** 101st Airborne Division SSI. **L.** First Allied Airborne Army SSI.

21. The First Ranger Battalion on a speed march in North Africa, January 1941. All are lightly equipped for moving far and fast. (US Army)

22. Men of the 29th Ranger Battalion training for the invasion of Europe in England, late 1943. Practice operation is against enemy strongpoints and the Ranger in the centre appears to be carrying a Bangalore Torpedo. (US Army)

23. (Overleaf) Rangers practising rough terrain amphibious landings in North Africa in December 1942. (US Army)

▲24 ▼25

24. Troops of the 82nd Airborne Division lift the tail of a glider so that equipment can be loaded through the nose. Note that these glider troops are armed with the M1A1 paratrooper carbine. (US Army)

25. Troops of a parachute artillery unit load their 75mm pack howitzer aboard a glider in 1943. (US Army)

26. Equipment with which an airborne light machine-gunner would jump. At the top are main and reserve parachutes. Below that is the tripod for the MG, lying on its padded drop bag, and a 125-round belt of ammunition. Other items of interest include an M1 rifle and a .45 automatic. Note that four 'blades' are carried: the M1905 bayonet; the Mk 1 knuckleduster trench knife (just behind the pistol); the M2 paratrooper's knife (just right of the compass), a 'switchblade' which the paratrooper could open with one hand if tangled in his lines to cut himself free; and the US Machete '18'. The presence of the machete indicates that this is the kit of a paratrooper in the Pacific Theatre of Operations, and this is borne out by the fact that it belongs to a member of the 503rd PIR. The three small bottles in the lower right-hand corner contain water purification tablets, salt tablets, and anti-fungus foot powder. A waterproof match container is just below the pocket knife. (US Army)

27. 'Glider-Riders' from the 320th Field Artillery Battalion, 82nd Airborne aboard their aircraft. Note the M1A1s with stocks folded and note also that for security reasons their shoulder sleeve insignia are covered. These glider troops do not appear to be wearing the paratroop trousers, which featured a large cargo pocket on the thigh; nor are they wearing the forked paratrooper chin strap on their helmets. (US Army)

28. Equipment carried when jumping by a demolition man of the 503rd Parachute Infantry Regiment. At the left is a rope in case a landing is made in the trees. The weapon is the 1928A1 Thompson SMG with a 50-round drum magazine in place. Spare 20-round magazines are carried on the belt. The demolition kit between the parachutes contains 18¼lb blocks of TNT, detonating cord, etc. (US Army)

26 ▲

27 ▲

◀31

29. During training in 1943, members of the joint American/Canadian 1st Special Service Force receive parachute instruction. The Force did not go through jump school at Fort Benning, but at Fort Harrison in Montana. It is thought that the 1st SSF, trained as paratroopers, commandos, ski troops, and mountain troops, were the toughest fighting unit of the Second World War. (US Army)

30. Troops of the 1st Special Service Force practise techniques of exiting from the aircraft at Fort Harrison. Although it is impossible to tell from this black-and-white photograph the men appear to be wearing OD utilities rather than the khaki ones associated with US paratroopers of the Second World War. (US Army)

31. MD assigned to the 1st SSF checks his medical equipment prior to a jump. (US Army)

▲32

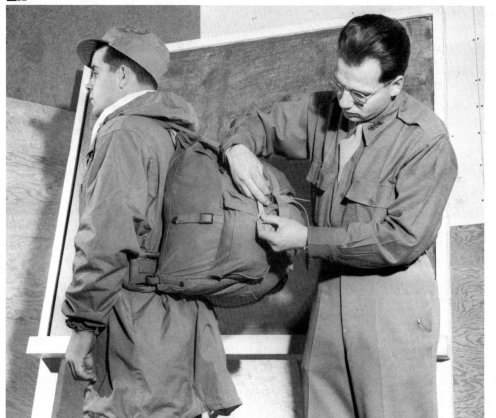

32. Troops of the 1st SSF, with static lines hooked up, wait to make their first jump. (US Army)

33. A soldier of the 1st SSF carrying the winter rucksack issued to troops of the Force and of the 10th Mountain Division for use in the mountains. If the hat and jacket appear somewhat Scandinavian in design it may be because ski instructors for the 1st SSF were former Norwegian ski troops and some US equipment was no doubt patterned on theirs. (US Army)

34. A soldier of the 1st SSF adjusts his skis after jumping in the mountains. He wears white camouflage parka and trousers and ski boots. The parachute in the background belongs to another jumper. (US Army)

◄**33**   **34**►

▲35 ▼36

35. Since they were being trained for operations in Alpine terrain, the radio men of the 1st SSF spent many hours practising in the Rockies. (US Army)
36. During early 1943 men of the 1st SSF perfect their skiing in preparation for what they thought might be a suicide mission. (US Army)
37. The effectiveness of the winter camouflage suit issued to the 1st SSF can be seen in this picture of a Force man with his M1. (US Army)

38. Canadian and US flags being lowered at Camp Harrison at sundown. Although originally US Force men wore US uniforms and Canadians wore Canadian uniforms, by the early months of 1943 the unit had been welded into a composite equipped with US uniforms, as can be seen from the Americans and Canadians in this photograph. (US Army)

39. Two of the four distinctive marks of the 1st SSF are visible in this photograph: the red arrowhead shoulder sleeve insignia with USA and CANADA in white letters and the red, white, and blue braided shoulder cord. The other two marks of the Force man were his parachutist's wings and the V-42 stiletto. Because of the confusion with Special Services, which provided entertainment for the troops, Force men often explained that they were special barbers trained to give front-line haircuts, and that the braid at the shoulders represented the barber's pole. Both Americans and Canadians, however, wore the braid and insignia with great pride, realizing that they were indeed an élite. (US Army)

40. Troops of the 1st SSF watch an officer demonstrating the correct technique for leaving an aircraft when making a parachute jump. All are wearing the knitted cap which was worn under the helmet in cold weather. (US Army)

◀38   39▲ 40▼

 41

41. Troops of the 1st SSF engage in a tug-of-war during training to develop strength. Note that their 'rope' is a length of parachute harness. (US Army)

42. Troops of the 1st SSF yell encouragement to some of their buddies emplaning for a jump. They are wearing the football-style crash helmet used during parachute training. (US Army)

▼**42**

43. In France, June 1944, a messenger uses a captured German cavalry horse. Unlike the paratroopers, the Rangers did not usually favour the M1 Carbine – many preferring instead the Springfield O3A3 rifle – but the Ranger in the left foreground is armed with one. (US Army)

44. On 12 June 1944, 82nd Airborne casualties are being evacuated by jeep. A Red Cross armband, worn by the 82nd medics on the left arm, is visible on at least two figures. The right arm was reserved for the US flag worn by the paratroopers who jumped during the Normandy invasion. (US Army)

45. A soldier of the 82nd Airborne passes a French civilian while moving inland on 8 June 1944. 82nd Airborne Division SSI and staff sergeant's rank are visible on his left sleeve. (US Army)

46. Men of the 10th Mountain Division set out on patrol in Italy in January 1945. Each man carries snowshoes. (US Army)

47. This staff sergeant of the 10th Mountain Division offers a good view of his divisional SSI and of the ice axe carried by the US 'Alpine troops'. Among the ribbons and decorations on his left breast are the combat infantryman's badge, bronze star, pre-Pearl Harbor Army Service ribbon, American Theater Ribbon, European Theater ribbon, and good conduct medal. (US Army)

▲45

▼46   47►

▲48 ▼49

48. Men of the 10th Mountain Division wearing long white camouflage overcoats load their packs into a Weasel tracked vehicle as they set out on patrol. The Weasel was originally intended for the 1st SSF, but actually saw more service with the 10th Mountain Division. (US Army)

49. Men of the 503rd Parachute Infantry Regiment after jumping to retake Corregidor Island in February 1945. The jump on the 'Rock' was one of the toughest of the war and was later commemorated in the regiment's shoulder sleeve insignia. Although many of the men taking part in this operation jumped with M1 Carbines these paratroopers carry the standard M1 Garand rifle. (US Army)

50. Some idea of the heavy bombardment which preceded the jump on Corregidor can be gained from the devastation visible in this photograph of men of the 503rd PIR moving down from 'Topside' towards the coast. (US Army)

50▼

51. Engineers from the 10th Mountain Division take cover behind a tank destroyer in Italy during March 1945. Although members of this division were issued with mountain climbing boots, the men seen here are wearing standard combat boots. (US Army)

52. Tenth Mountain Division medics with a casualty in Italy early in 1945. Note that the helmets also bear the Red Cross as well as the armbands. The uniform is the OD jacket and trousers which began to be issued in 1943. (US Army)

53. Troops of the 10th Mountain Division advance through the Sassomolare area of Italy in March 1945. Note that the linings for the battle jackets are still being worn because of the cold in the higher areas. (US Army)

◄**51**

▲54

54. This photograph of the jump on Corregidor gives some idea of the difficulty of the operation. The boat in the foreground is on station to pick up paratroopers who land in the water. (US Army)
55. Men of the 17th Airborne Division prepare to move out after the jump across the Rhine in March 1945. American flags were used for identification in this operation as they had been on D-Day. The purpose of the scarves worn by the two men in the centre is unknown, but it was probably a company or battalion recognition sign. (US Army)
56. Men of the 10th Mountain Division relax at their staging area near Pisa in January 1945. A GI duffle bag is clearly visible in front

of the soldier in the foreground. This is a good indication that the men are in a rear area since duffle bags would not normally be carried during combat. The weapon on the ground appears to be an M1 Carbine. Technician 4th Grade insignia is clearly visible on the folded jacket in the foreground. Both OD and white socks are drying on the tent. The white socks were probably worn under the GI socks. (US Army)
57. Troops of Battery B, 616th Pack Howitzer Battalion, 10th Mountain Division, carrying 75mm ammunition during the bombardment of German positions near Vincinetta in February 1945. (US Army)

▼55

▲58

▲59

60 ▲

◄61   62 ▲

58. Engineers from the 10th Mountain Division built this tramway for the evacuation of wounded down the mountainside of Mt. Serrasiccia. (US Army)

59. Tramway built by the 126th Mountain Engineers being used by artillery observers. (US Army)

60. Tenth Mountain Division engineers sweeping for mines in the Mt. Della Torraccia area in February 1945. The power pack for the mine detector is worn on the back. (US Army)

61. Men of the 10th Mountain Division laying down covering fire while men of their unit advance along the Porretta Moderna Highway. The man on the left is armed with a .30 Browning LMG; the man on the right appears to be carrying the mountain rucksack. For ski duty the rucksack would be white and would contain: extra socks and sweater; ski repair kit and extra aluminium ski tip; emergency medical kit including elastic bandages in case of a sprain; wax, paraffin, and cork for maintenance of skis; silk sectional tent and collapsible stove; sleeping bag, soap, toothbrush, and comb, full camouflage dress (white), compass and maps. In Alpine regions it would also contain: ice-axe, crampons, rope, ice-pitons, avalanche cord. (US Army)

62. Men of the 513th PIR, 17th Airborne Division, 1st Allied Airborne Army, assemble after landing near Wesel after the jump across the Rhine in March 1945. The helmet and Sten Mk V SMG readily identify the figure in the left foreground as a British paratrooper. Of interest is the fact that the American paratroopers attach their first aid kit to the front of the helmet while the British paratroopers affix theirs to the back. The paratrooper's Y-chinstrap is very evident on the trooper crouching behind the jeep. His US flag on the right sleeve is to identify him to the local population. (US Army)

63. This photograph of Major-General Miley, CO of the 17th Airborne Division (left), offers a good view of the quick-release box for the parachute. Just below it he carries field-glasses in a case. Note also the first aid kit worn on his helmet. The brigadier-general, on the right, wears the SSI of the 1st Allied Airborne Army. The photograph was taken in March 1945 as the 17th Airborne was preparing for the Rhine crossing. (US Army)

64. Glider troops of the 17th Airborne Division marching to their aircraft in preparation for the jump across the Rhine. (US Army)

65. Men of the 194th Glider Infantry have just ignited with machine-gun fire the hay in a barn harbouring a sniper. The 194th was part of the 17th Airborne Division and this photograph was taken in March 1945 during the assault across the Rhine. Since the glider troops landed with jeeps the troops shown here are travelling very light, their equipment being carried in the jeeps. (US Army)

▲63 ▼64

▲66

66. Troops of the 10th Mountain Division marching German prisoners to a stockade in Italy in April 1945. Note the bandolier with spare M1 Garand clips worn by the man in the right foreground. The prisoners are tagged with information about them and where they were captured. It was not unknown for the members of CIC (Counter-Intelligence Corps) who interrogated such prisoners to imply that those among them who proved uncooperative would be handed over to the Russian Red Army. (US Army)

67. Men of the 110th Signal Company, 10th Mountain Division, string wire as the division advances near Camidello, Italy in April 1945. (US Army)

▼67

68. ▲

68. Troops of the 10th Mountain Division march a long string of German POWs into captivity in April 1945. (US Army)

69. Men of the 17th Airborne Division prepare for the jump across the Rhine. Note that the two general officers standing in the centre both carry their 1911A1 .45 automatics in the GI shoulder holster. The straps around the legs were used to lash equipment close to the body while jumping. The quick-release box for the parachute harness can be clearly seen (man standing at the right, the man standing second from the left, and the man kneeling second from the left). The ripcord handle on the reserve chute (man kneeling on the left) is also clearly visible in this photograph. (US Army)

69. ▼

◀70

71▲

70. General Maxwell Taylor and Winston Churchill inspect the 101st Airborne Division in England in March 1944. Note the M36 cartridge belt on the man in the right foreground. Note also that General Taylor wears his paratroop cap badge on his sidecap. Officers wore this badge on the right (the wearer's right) side of the sidecap so that rank insignia could be worn on the left side. Enlisted personnel wore the badge on the left side. (US Army)

71. Major-General Maxwell Taylor, CO of the 101st Airborne Division, receiving the DSM from General Jacob Devers. The medal was awarded in May 1945. Note that General Taylor's parachutist's wings are worn on his left breast. On his left sleeve he wears the 101st Airborne SSI and near the cuff four service bars, each indicating six months of overseas service during the war. (US Army)

72. Major-General James Gavin reviews men of the 82nd Airborne Division which he commanded in June 1945. (US Army)

72 ▶

73. Self-propelled artillery of the 10th Mountain Division firing near Gargnano in April 1945. (US Army)

▲74 ▼75

74. Troops of the 101st Airborne Division help their CO, Major-General Maxwell Taylor, check his parachute prior to the jump in Holland. A respirator container is visible on General Taylor's left hip. The large cargo pockets on the paratroop trousers can be seen on the sergeant at the right, who wears his paratrooper's cap insignia on the left side indicating that he is an enlisted man. (US Army)

75. A soldier of the 1st Special Service Force in a concealed position takes aim with his M41 Johnson light machine-gun which was a good weapon for the Force because of its lightness.

Note that the magazine is located on the left side of the receiver. This man is wearing the parka with wolf's fur fringe issued for cold weather. (US Army)

76. Brigadier-General James Gavin checks his equipment before emplaning for the jump over Holland. Note the baggy paratrooper's trousers with large cargo pocket. Note also that General Gavin wears his .45 automatic in the conventional GI hip holster and carries a full-sized Garand rifle rather than an M1 carbine. (US Army)

▲77 ▼78

77. General James Gavin briefs men of his 82nd Airborne Division in September 1944 in preparation for the airborne assault on Holland in Operation 'Market Garden'. Note Gavin's highly polished boots. More than one 'rear area commando' caught wearing paratrooper boots by the tough men of the airborne divisions had them removed forcibly. (US Army)

78. Men of the 10th Mountain Division moving along paths blasted through a minefield in April 1945. (US Army)

79. Brigadier-General David Ruffner of the 10th Mountain Division watches his men advance through the Po Valley late in April 1945. Note that only the single star on the shoulder of his jacket denotes that he is a general officer. (US Army)

80. Men of the 17th Airborne Division attempt to warm up after the jump across the Rhine. Note that the PFC on the right wears the 17th Airborne's 'Talon From Heaven' on his jacket, and instead of the normal paratroop boots appears to be wearing overshoes. The man at the left has an M3 Trench Knife strapped to his right leg. This method of carrying the M3 was popular with US airborne troops, being out of the way while jumping, but handy if lines needed to be cut. This same trooper is armed with a Bazooka. (US Army)

79 ▶

80 ▼

▲81 ▼82

83▲

81. Men of the 462nd Airborne Artillery are pinned down by Japanese machine-gun fire while trying to assemble their pack howitzers after jumping over Corregidor in February 1945. (US Army)

82. Men of the 513th PIR advancing on Munster in April 1945. Note the folding stock M1A1 carbine carried by the paratrooper in the left foreground. He carries either an M3 Trench Knife or M4 bayonet strapped to his leg in typical paratrooper fashion. (US Army)

83. Men of the 1st SSF prepare their close-quarters weapons while retaking the Aleutians from the Japanese. The man in the left foreground appears to have a .45 automatic; the man at the right is sharpening the famous V-42 stiletto of the Force. SSI worn by the man with the V-42 is that of the Kiska Task Force. Woollen caps were very popular with the 1st SSF who had been trained for Arctic operations. (US Army)

84. These men of the 101st Airborne jumped into Normandy on D-Day. They are seen here eating their first proper meal in 17 days, after having evaded German patrols in order to link up with advancing American troops. The name 'LEGS' appearing on the utility jacket and cap of the man second from the right is more typical of the Vietnam War, but paratroopers were allowed rather more leeway when in action because of the élite nature of their units. (US Army)

84▼

▲85

85. In February 1945, men of the 616th Mountain Artillery Battalion prepare to load their pack howitzer during the fighting in Italy. (US Army)

86. USMC gliders taking off on a training operation at Parris Island in 1941. (USMC)

▼86

87. Men of the 2nd Marine Raider Battalion man a .30 MG in a flooded foxhole on Bougainville during 1943. These Raiders wear the camouflage helmet cover, so typical of the US Marines, and full combat pack. Both the helmet and the green utilities worn by the Marines were virtually the same as those of the Army in the Pacific, though the Raiders normally wore the spotted camouflage utilities. (USMC)

88. USMC dog handlers, attached to the 2nd Marine Raider Regiment, take cover on Bougainville in December 1943. Marine 'Devil Dogs' were attached to the Raiders who normally scouted ahead. Each of these handlers is equipped with an M1 Carbine. (USMC)

88▼

▲89

89. Marine Raiders struggling through the mud on Bougainville in November 1943. (USMC)

90. Marine Raiders in their rubber boats head ashore for a mission in the South Pacific. (USMC)

91. These Marine Raiders on Bougainville in November 1943, offer a good view of their spotted camouflage utilities. Note that the man on the right also wears the camouflaged utility hat. (USMC)

92. The V-42 stiletto carried by members of the 1st Special Service Force. The V-42 was based on the F-S knife of the British Commandos, but incorporated the 'fingerprint' on the ricasso, supposedly to remind the Force men where to put their thumb when delivering a thrust to the carotid artery. Note also the pointed skull crusher incorporated into the pommel.

93. The OSS version of the F-S stiletto. The knife was completely devoid of markings so that its origin could not be traced, and used a sheath whose frog was fabricated from a pancake-turner.

▼90

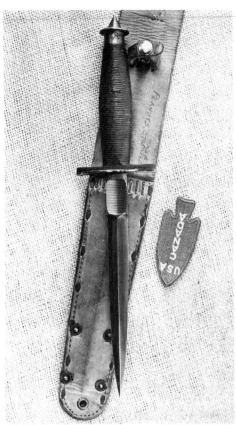

91▲ 92▲ 93▼

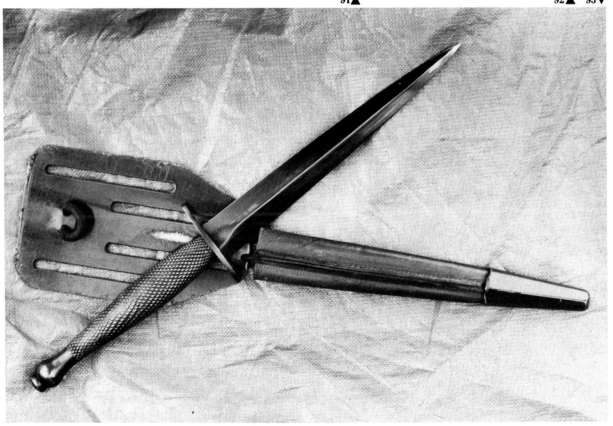

▲ 94 ▼ 95

94. These men of the 1st SSF, encamped in the mountains, offer a good view of the cold weather parka which was issued to them. (US Army)

95. Marine Raiders and paratroopers during a raid on Bougainville late in November 1943. The man in the lower foreground appears to be armed with a Reising Model 50 SMG. (USMC)

96. Late in the summer of 1943 these Marine Raiders dive for their foxholes as Japanese aircraft attack. Note that they wear the spotted camouflage pattern used by the Marines in the Pacific. (USMC)

96▼

▲97 ▼98

97. US Marine Raiders and Para-Marines returning the fire of Japanese snipers, having landed eight miles behind Japanese lines on Bougainville at the end of November 1943. (USMC)

98. Marine Raiders on Bougainville equipped for combat give a good idea of the typical kit carried by this élite Marine unit. Note the machetes worn by the men on the right. (USMC)

99. Marine Raiders return from night patrol on Bougainville in which they were ordered to dig foxholes out in front of Marine positions and to use only their knives to kill any Japanese encountered. Nevertheless, they were well supplied with ammunition for their M1 rifles as can be seen from the bandoliers worn by many of the men. (USMC)

100. Marine Raiders with their scout dogs moving through the jungle on Bougainville. The man sitting down at the left has a .30 Browning MG, while the man second from the left carries ammunition boxes of additional belts for the MG. (USMC)

99 ▲   100 ▼

▲101 ▼102

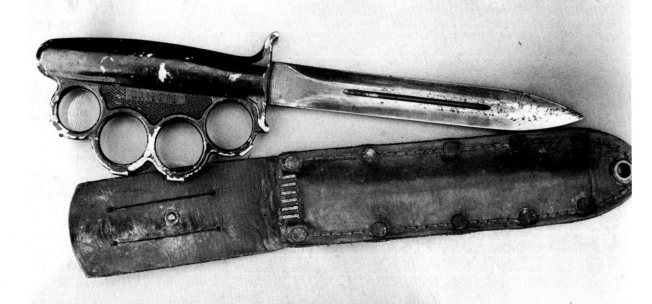

66

103▲

101. The Marine Raider stiletto was created especially for this Marine raiding force and was based on the F-S Commando dagger. Other knives carried by the Raiders included the famous USMC Ka-Bar (middle) and the M3 Trench Knife (right) which was also popular with the Army's paratroopers. (USMC)

102. The Everett Knuckle Knife was also popular with many paratroopers.

103. One of the least known élite units of the Second World War was a joint allied airborne unit destined to parachute into POW camps ahead of advancing troops to save prisoners from execution or elimination. Note that the two American members (middle) wear British parachutist's wings on their left cuffs and below them the special insignia of their unit. The US sergeant wears his cap insignia on the incorrect side for an enlisted man. In fact, the other US member appears to be an officer who is wearing his cap insignia on the enlisted side. There would be some temptation to think that the photograph has been reversed, but the Frenchman (third from left) wears his Free French para wings on the right breast which is correct. Perhaps the unit has been celebrating and the two Americans have got their hats mixed up.

104. Early in the development of airborne troops within the US Army this photograph was taken (obviously posed) of troops undergoing glider training. Note that the old First World War style of helmet is still being worn. (US Air Force)

104▼

105. US Marine paratrooper shows two points of special interest in his equipment. His weapon is the Reising Model 55 SMG which was issued to the Marine paras. Note also the elbow pads used by the Marine paratroopers but soon eliminated. (IWM)